IN TIME'S RIFT

WAVE BOOKS / SEATTLE AND NEW YORK

ERNST MEISTER
IN TIME'S RIFT

///

TRANSLATED BY GRAHAM FOUST AND SAMUEL FREDERICK

PUBLISHED BY WAVE BOOKS

WWW.WAVEPOETRY.COM

WAVE BOOKS TITLES ARE DISTRIBUTED TO THE TRADE BY

CONSORTIUM BOOK SALES AND DISTRIBUTION

PHONE: 800-283-3572 / SAN 631-760X

THIS TITLE IS AVAILABLE IN LIMITED EDITION HARDCOVER

DIRECTLY FROM THE PUBLISHER

LIBRARY OF CONGRESS CATALOGING-IN-PUBLICATION DATA

MEISTER, ERNST, 1911–1979

[IM ZEITSPALT. ENGLISH]

IN TIME'S RIFT : POEMS = IM ZEITSPALT / BY ERNST MEISTER ;

TRANSLATED BY GRAHAM FOUST AND SAMUEL FREDERICK. — 1ST ED.

P. CM.

ISBN 978-1-933517-62-9 (ALK. PAPER)

I. FOUST, GRAHAM W., 1970– II. FREDERICK, SAMUEL.

III. TITLE. IV. TITLE: IM ZEITSPALT.

PT2625.E322I413 2012

831—DC23

2011050617

DESIGNED AND COMPOSED BY QUEMADURA

PRINTED IN THE UNITED STATES OF AMERICA

9 8 7 6 5 4 3 2 1

FIRST EDITION

INTRODUCTION

Ernst Meister had already begun writing poetry, prose, and
dramatic works when, having just turned nineteen, he en-
rolled as a theology student at the University of Marburg in
the winter semester of 1930. He soon traded his theological
pursuits for philosophy, literature, and art history, attending
lectures by Karl Löwith and Hans-Georg Gadamer, two of
Martin Heidegger's former students, both of whom, along
with their teacher, had a tremendous impact on Meister's
work. Later he began working under Löwith on a dissertation
on Nietzsche, a project he eventually abandoned because of
Löwith's forced exile, though by that time he had already pub-
lished his first collection of verse, *Ausstellung* (Exhibition),
which appeared in 1932.

When Adolf Hitler became chancellor early the next year,
Germany's literary landscape changed drastically, and Meis-
ter's work (compared in an early review to the painting of
Wassily Kandinsky) was considered too abstract for the new,
neoclassical aesthetics of the Third Reich, which branded any
hint of experimentation as "degenerate." Though Meister
composed poetry after 1933, he gave up trying to publish it.
This renunciation lasted two full decades—only three short
prose pieces would appear in the feuilletons of the *Frank-*

furter Zeitung in 1935. During the Second World War, he suffered a series of protracted illnesses and was called to military service twice. He first served at a railroad artillery in Rügenwalde (in present-day Poland), where he was injured and deemed unfit for combat; during his second tour of duty, he was deployed to Stalingrad, though he and his division never made it there. After another period of illness and additional military service in France, Meister ended up in Italy, where he was captured by the Americans and held as a prisoner of war. Upon his release, he returned to Hagen (in what was to become West Germany), where, in relative isolation, he worked in his father's railroad clamp factory and continued to write.

Eight years after the war, Meister published his second book of poems (1953's *Unterm schwarzen Schafspelz* [Under Black Sheep's Clothing]), and after eight more years he would dedicate himself exclusively to his writing. By the 1960s, he had published over a half dozen volumes of verse, though he failed to attract the same recognition as contemporaries such as Karl Krolow, Günter Eich, or Paul Celan. Meister was, in fact, an outsider—and not by choice. He was never asked to join the Gruppe 47, a collective of over 200 writers who represented—and effectively determined—the literary establishment in the postwar years. But neither was his work embraced once that group's influence had waned, after the student revolutions of 1968. In this period of political agitation, Meister's verse was largely perceived as apolitical and nihilistic, and therefore unsuited to the prevailing literary climate.

Like the American poet George Oppen (1908–1984)—
who also fought in the Second World War (though on a differ-
ent side and under very different circumstances) and who
stopped publishing poetry for a prolonged period before, dur-
ing, and after it—Meister takes much stock in "the little
words," words that often prove crucial to his efforts to, as Op-
pen says, "lay down the substantive for its own sake." The fol-
lowing couplet from one of the poems from this book seems
emblematic of Meister's style, and it's fair to say that these
lines wouldn't be out of place in one of Oppen's poems:

> I look at a window,
> square of sky.

How many poems in which the speaker looks *out* a window
have been written? How many in which the speaker looks *at*
one? If the average speaker-near-a-window poem tries to sat-
isfy and/or surprise us with what's beyond the window, Meis-
ter's poem catches us off guard by its speaker's stopping just
short of making use of that aperture and then renaming it.
Here, we're not so taken with *what* the speaker sees; rather,
we're drawn to *how* he sees—and how unusual it is to see
someone see (and say) in such a way.

* * *

Recognition finally came for Meister, though almost too late.
He died just two days after receiving word that his life's work
would be honored with a Georg Büchner Prize, the most pres-

tigious literary award in Germany, which was then granted him posthumously, a fitting tribute for a poet so preoccupied with mortality. To be sure, death is often Meister's subject, and yet a slight ontological shift permits us to see him as a poet of *life*, a writer who chronicles what it means to live with the fact that he (and you) will at some point cease to be. That Meister is frequently compared to Celan is, in this respect, perhaps inevitable, even more so given their shared predilection for terse, "hermetic" verse that seems to approach the limits of the language. Meister's poems, however, do not exhibit Celan's deep ambivalence toward—indeed, distrust of—language itself; he thus rarely resorts to the kinds of contorted neologisms that characterize Celan's verse, especially that of his late period. Furthermore, Meister is not particularly interested in historical time. His poems rarely refer to actual occurrences or places, but instead explore the abstract, metaphysical spaces opened up by eternity, the awareness of which Meister figures as something terrifying.

This horror in the face of the infinite is one of the main themes of *Im Zeitspalt* (*In Time's Rift*), Meister's penultimate collection, and the midpoint of an informal trilogy constituting his "late work." (The full volume was published in 1976, though all but three of the poems in the book's first half appeared in bibliophile editions in 1969 and 1973.) The book's title alludes to Pascal's *Pensées*, in which the mathematician and philosopher considers the short span of his life "swallowed up in the eternity before and after." Rather than facing eternity as something edifying, Pascal is frightened by being "engulfed in the infinite immensity of spaces." Meister seizes on this notion as an expression of our existential condition. In his posthumous papers he identifies our brief life as "time's rift," which he then defines as "conscious time between two eternities." Elsewhere Meister expands on this idea, with direct reference to Pascal: "Between an 'eternity before' and an 'eternity after' . . . we have our life's term. In a rift of time the corner of the universe appears to consciousness. —An unfathomability without compare." Consciousness of the infinite cosmos forces us to attend to consciousness of our own frightening world, and, in turn, to confront our mortality. The infinite is the correlate of the nothingness that is our fate. But this nothingness—which, according to Heidegger, "itself nothings" ("Das Nichts selbst nichtet")—is not just a void in which we lose ourselves. Nothingness, and the death that leads to it, grants the world meaning, and also makes poetry possible. In a gloss on one of this book's poems, "He, the monosyllabic one," Meister makes this sentiment explicit: "Death is the extinction of existence through which I first come to understand world at all. It even brings forth poetry (the line of verse) . . ."

Like much of Meister's late verse, *In Time's Rift* is shot through with traces of his predecessors—the cadences of Rilke, the stark, metaphysical landscapes of Trakl, and the tortured syntax of Hölderlin can be found throughout. Meister's penchant for grand abstractions and philosophical concepts, often taken directly from thinkers such as Hegel, Schopenhauer, Nietzsche, and of course Heidegger, forces his readers to attend to the modulations of thought over image. This persistently pulls his language into the realm of thinking, an activity made extraordinarily intense by the taut, afflicted space opened up by the poem, a space analogous to life. Consider this short poem from near the end of the book:

> You see yourself
> as a stranger
> often,
> for before long
> you'll drip
> with rot,
> appear to rest.

What makes the poem work—what makes one want to say it again and again—is that its use of the word "for" (*denn* in the German) to yoke a familiar fiction to a future certainty allows the reader to feel his or her brief time on ancient Earth in a new way. On the one hand, the word "for" could indicate that the poem's "you" sees himself as a stranger by way of his regularly picturing himself as a corpse, a thing he isn't (yet). On the other hand, "for" also suggests that the you's seeing himself as a stranger—whatever particular visions that might entail—is something he does now precisely because he'll be unable to do so when dead. In either case, the eventual fact of death stimulates the you's imagination, and the poem as a whole enables its readers' imaginations to oscillate between —and pull together—these two possibilities, the first of which feels grisly but familiar, the second of which feels empowering but odd. Given that the you only *appears* to rest in his state of busy decomposition—and so continues to participate posthumously in the act of artifice—it's also possible to read the poem as a kind of prescient and backhanded ars poetica.

American readers new to Meister will find that *In Time's Rift* shares many concerns with those of a large handful of twentieth-century American poets, particularly Wallace Stevens (see his "Less and Less Human, O Savage Spirit" and "Flyer's Fall"), Laura Riding (see many of her "Poems of Immediate Occasion"), William Bronk (see his "How It Diminishes Us" and "Real Thinking"), and Robert Creeley (see his "The Window" and "The Farm"), though it may be that the experience of reading Meister for the first time is most akin to one's initial encounters with Emily Dickinson, whose poems, like Meister's, at once entice and irritate the mouth and mind. (Indeed, we have attempted to retain as many irritants as possible in our translations—including Meister's often unnatural syntax—which we feel are a large part of what makes this work attractive.) Consider the opening of Dickinson's poem 1462, the mixed tenses of which resemble those of "Did you, sun, thieve," this volume's final verse:

> We knew not that we were to live—
> Nor when—we are to die—

Later in Dickinson's poem—which ultimately makes the claim that both God and life are felt as intrusions (as opposed, we suppose, to inclusions)—she refers to our ignorance as a piece of armor ("our cuirass") and asserts that we wear our mortality "as an Option Gown" until asked to remove it. Like Dickinson's, Meister's sizable body of work is the record of a humble and valiant attempt to put a chink (*ein Spalt*) in our not-knowing, however resistant or protective that not-knowing may be.

In introductions to books like the one you're holding, translators often make a point of discussing at length the particular difficulties presented to them by their attempts to wrangle a poem from one language into another. While such discussions can prove both compelling and helpful, it's also very likely that anyone who has ever tried to translate a poem would admit that a list of the simplicities associated with such a task is virtually nonexistent. Translation is impossible, and yet, as Gertrude Stein writes, "Why do something if it can be done." We'd like to think that Ernst Meister, whose poems attempt to talk us through the impossible—or, rather, try to talk us right up to it—would have appreciated our efforts. It's our hope that our readers will as well.

GRAHAM FOUST AND SAMUEL FREDERICK

Und was
will diese Sonne
uns, was

springt
aus enger Pforte
jener großen Glut?

Ich weiß
nichts Dunkleres
denn das Licht.

And what
does this sun want
with us, what

leaps
from the strait gate
of that huge glow?

I know
no greater darkness
than the light.

Wir hatten
Spielwerk,
wir hatten, von Namen,
Tod, den
unerlebbaren Punkt, wir
hatten Sprache—aber
gab es Wir?

Es gab
aus einer Begattung,
aus Ich und Ich ein
Drittes, ein
Allgemeines womöglich;
wärs der Verlust?

Spielwerk, ich sahs
entschweben,
es richtete sich auf mich
Sterben, es
deutete, mich entsetzend,
Sprache auf ihren Mund

. . .

We had
toy clockwork,
we had, of name,
death, the
unexperienceable point, we
had language—but
was there We?

There was
from a coupling,
from I and I a
third, a
universal, possibly;
would that be loss?

Clockwork, I watched it
float away,
dying
aimed itself at me,
language, shocking me,
pointed at its mouth

. . .

Da ich nicht weiß,
was ich bin
von zu Haus,
muß ich
Gedanke sein.

Von niemand
gestoßen,
verrätselt sich
Sein
in sich selbst.

Since I don't know
what I am
from home,
I must
be thought.

Jostled
by no one,
being
riddles itself
into itself.

Er, der Einsilbige,
dreimal ein Buchstab,
macht, wofern nicht
Unglück ist, vollkommenes,
einen Verstand. (Das hat
einer von uns gesagt.)
Er macht die Zeile, so daß
Lebendiges sich sieht
im Gehn.

He, the monosyllabic one,

five times a letter,

makes, insofar as there

is no misfortune, complete,

an understanding. (This

according to one of us.)

He forms a line so that

the living sees itself

as it shuffles off.

ER ist ER, obwohl
einzig ein Wort,
Erbe der Zeugenden. Er
entspringt, wenn ich falle,
ganz beraubt, vom
Rücken der Tierheit.—
Ich sei nun getroffen oder
verwelkt, ER ist,
Wort aller Worte, ein
Leeres in mir.

HE is HE, though
only a word,
heir of those who procreate. He
leaps forth, when I fall,
entirely robbed, from
beastliness's back.—
Whether I'm now struck or
shriveled, HE is,
word of all words, a
blank in me.

DER zeichnet Mücken
in die Luft. Der schreibt
die Schwalbe, Fängerin,
mir in die Augen. Der
läßt dich schreiben. Der,
ziemlich hell, streicht durch.

Der streicht den Schreiber durch,
wenn es der Tag ist.

THIS ONE sketches gnats
in air. This one writes
the swallow, gnat catcher,
in my eyes. This one
has you written. This one,
rather bright, crosses out.
He crosses the writer out,
when the day comes.

Das
Geschriebene, das
geschrieben Gemalte,
gleich der Spirale,
träumerisch,
das, was ich tu,
solang ich mit den Sinnen
begreife.

Aber kurz
ist die Zeit.
Grabher
befremdet dich oft
die eigene Hand.

Und:
ein Törichtes,
fragst du, was denn,
zerstöbe einst
dieser Stern und
der schreckliche Plan,
worin doch
das Herz gewesen,
die Frucht aller Früchte
sei.

The
written, the
drawn, written,
like a spiral—
dreamlike,
that which I do,
so long as I take hold
with my senses.

But time
is short.
Graved here,
your own hand often
looks strange to you.

And:
something foolish,
you ask, what then,
if this star and
the terrible plan,
wherein, nonetheless,
the heart lay,
were to vaporize,
would the fruit of all fruits
be.

Sage: nach Aas
und Rosen
dufte der Begriff,

er sei
und habe Tag
und schlafe

unter
dem eigenen Dach,
so Herr wie Knecht.

Say: may the concept
smell of carrion
and roses;

may it be
and have day
and sleep

beneath
its own roof,
as much master as slave.

Gesang, ein
Ähnliches dem, das war
oder ein anderes—
und ich weiß doch
um nicht Singendes.

Nein, ich meine
nicht Steine, Blumen,
das Tier, sondern, menschlich,
die im ganz fertigen
Ungeschick, wonach

es gibt
Leiden,
vom Leiden allein
dessen Das.

Song, something
similar to what was
or another—
and I do know
of what does not sing.

No, I don't mean
stones, flowers,
beast, but rather, humanly,
those in the fully completed
blunder, whereby

there is
suffering,
from suffering alone
its That.

Altes Klagen,
frühes Klagen
sagt:
Du sollst mich klagen.

Schön
tut mir ein Blütenzweig.
Klag es, altes,
frühes Klagen!

Tritt hinzu
im Harnisch einer,
will, daß ich
das alte, frühe
Klagen klage.

Spricht mirs vor,
ich sprech die Worte
frühen Klagens,
alten Klagens.

Ihre Wahrheit,
ich erbrech sie
über jenen
Blütenzweig.

Old lamenting,
early lamenting
says:
you should lament me.

A budding sprig
flatters me.
Lament it, old,
early lamenting!

Stepping up
in armor, someone
wants me
to lament the old, early
lamenting;

recites it for me—
I speak the words
of early lamenting,
old lamenting.

Its truth—
I vomit it
over that
budding sprig.

Hier
solche Waage.

Die eine der Schalen
bedrängt
von einem Blatte
des Mohnkelchs,

von hinsiechenden
Kindes Atem
die andere.

Von so
ratlosen Zungen
heimgesucht
unser Wesen.

Here
such scales.

One of the trays
beset
by a sepal
from a poppy;

by the breath
of a languishing child,
the other.

By such
bewildered pointers
plagued—
our being.

Und ich grüße
alle die Verwirrung
schiefen Hauptes,

wenn er blutet blutet
auf ein
Tönendes, der Tropfen.

Gibts noch anderes
Ohr dafür
als deines?

Kein Gehör
haust
außerhalb der Erde.

Wo ich geh
und steh, er
blutet blutet

auf ein
Tönendes,
der Tropfen.

And I salute
the whole confusion
with head askew,

when it drips blood drips blood
on a
resonant body, the drop.

Is there an ear
for that other
than yours?

No sense of hearing
has a home
beyond the earth.

Wherever I walk
or stop, it
drips blood drips blood

on a
resonant body,
the drop.

»Unter dem tiefsten Flügel
der ältesten Taube«
verbirgt sich
der Gegensinn,
widerlaufend dem Schlage.
Wo das Älteste ist,
sitzt Verneinung im Neste,
gramäugig unermeßlich.

"In the deepest reaches
of the oldest dove's wing"
countersense
conceals itself,
going at the blow.
Where the oldest squab is,
negation sits in the nest,
grief-eyed beyond measure.

Es geschieht aber
in unsicherer Richtung
ein Ruck. Ein Haken
wendet den Flug des Vogels.

Der Gezweifelte
scheint im Glück
und schießt
auf ein Irdisches zu.

But it happens:
in an uncertain direction
a jerk. A crook
changes the flight of the bird.
The one doubted
gleams in fortune
and hurtles
toward something earthly.

Aphrodite, der Name,
mögliche Kontur,
Körper, vorm Himmel
ruhend auf einer Mauer am See.

Gut, daß ichs sah,
begierig (wissend
von Ungestalt), die Erde
als Meisterin zu erkennen
durch den Zufallswurf.

So als krönte sich
mit diesem, ohne Mut,
doch hoch erfinderisch,
die Todeswelt.

Aphrodite, the name,
possible contour,
body in repose against the sky
on a wall by the sea.

Good thing I noticed this,
eager (aware
of misshapenness) to recognize
Earth as master craftswoman
by dint of the random toss.

As if with this, without courage,
but with great innovation,
the world of death
crowned itself.

Eine Mahlzeit
war essend; es lagen
Sonne und Mond
in der Schüssel.

Du
mir entgegen im Scheine.
Staub
umschwebte uns zärtlich.

There was an eating
meal; in the bowl
there lay
sun and moon.

We
had a face-off in the light.
Dust
floated around us, tenderly.

»Ton, der über dem Tode

schwebt mit Gewichten,

gehalten von oben dem Pol

und unten dem Erdkern« . . .

Dies gesetzt,

verwölkt das Bewußtstein,

und von Pein träuft Öl

gegen den Schlaf hin.

Diesem Blut dann

laß seinen Zirkel

und dem Hirn, das es lenkt,

sein Weltvergessen.

Es gibt Bilder genug

aus dem blickenden Anfang.

"Sound that hovers over
death with weights,
held from above by the pole
and from below by Earth's core" . . .

Given that,
consciousness clouds up,
and from pain oil drips
down toward sleep.

To this blood, then,
leave its bow compass,
and to the brain, which it steers,
its forgetting of world.

There are images enough
from the glimpsing beginning.

Wie denn soll

ein Gehirn und Gebein,

wer weiß, wie

entstanden, ihr Blumen,

sich bequemen in der

Sternstraße, wo es

sich übertrinkt

an der unbenambaren

Milch und sich höchst leidlich

davon entbindet,

ein Aas—

How then should
a brain and bone,
produced how, who
knows, you flowers,
adapt in the
street of stars, where it
overdrinks
on unnamable
milk and most sufferably
births itself from it,
a carcass—

Dies gibts
von verwandten Leuten
zu sehn:

die ebene Fläche,
vom Gärtner gemacht,
Vater und Mutter zum Beispiel,

grabsäuberlich,
Leben beglichen.
Ach, der Gedankensohn.

Of those
related to one another
this can be seen:

the even surface,
made by the gardener,
father and mother for instance,

tidy as a grave,
life squared away.
Oh, the son of thinking.

II

Ach, in der
eigenen, ach,
in der Todeshaut . . .

Wir haben,
wenn wir uns wissen,
nur einigermaßen
gewonnen,
denn das Treiben geschieht
im Rücken, niemand
kommt hinter sich.

Da vorn
ist das Grab.

Wie die Luft
ein Geranke bewegt,
Blumen sich regen,
damit sind innen
manchmal
die Augen befaßt.

Oh, in one's
own, oh,
in death's skin . . .

We've only,
if we have a sense of ourselves,
to some degree
come out ahead,
because the push comes
in the back, no one
can get behind himself.

Up ahead
is the grave.

How the air
moves a tendril,
flowers stir—
this is what sometimes
concerns
the eyes inside.

Was uns
verheißen ist,
uns blutig Geborenen:
der Ungram
nach der geringen Zeit,
anstößig
dem Lebenshaupt.

What is
promised us,
we who were born bloody:
ungrief
after the dwindled time,
offensive
to the living head.

Lang oder kurz ist die Zeit,
und das Wahre,
das sich ereignen wird,
heißt Sterben.

Danach bist du
gleichsinnig mit
der Erde, dem Himmel,
die sich nicht wissen.
(Aber wer bist du noch?)

Was eigentlich hieß denn das:
geboren, Zeit zu gebären
im Unterfangen des Bewußtseins—
wozu »ich«?

Time is long or short,
and the truth
that will transpire
is called dying.

Thereafter you're
accordant with
the earth, the heavens,
who have no sense of themselves.
(But who are you then?)

So what did it really mean:
born to give birth to time
in the endeavor we call consciousness—
what is "I" for?

Dies, das Vertraute,
wird dir auf ewig sein
ein Unbekanntes,
bist dir ja selber
nicht mehr bekannt.

This, the familiar,
will eternally be
an unknown to you;
anyway, you're no longer
known to yourself.

Niemand, der war,
weiß noch je
etwas von Sein.
Auch Ewigkeit
ist ihm nicht Gegenwart.
Das Begrifflose blüht
fern gestorbenem Sinn.

No one who ever was
knows anything yet
about being.
Even eternity
is not the present for him.
What's conceptless blooms
far from meaning that's deceased.

So wie du gemacht bist,

von Natur Natur,

worin anscheinend

der Fremdling wohnt

als Widersprecher des Zwanges,

wirst du im Himmel,

seiner Leere, verschwinden,

vom Denken los, dem Geringsten.

Dahinten, vorbei das

hochbuckelnde Tier,

sich sträubend vorm Rande.

Das Hinüber, wärs denn

kein Katzensprung?

In the same way that you're made,

by nature nature,

wherein the stranger

seems to live

as contradictor of constraint,

so in heaven,

its void, you'll disappear,

free of thinking, the most trifling thing.

Back there, passing by, the

high-bucking beast,

rearing up in the face of the brink.

Crossing over would be

a mere stone's throw, no?

Sei du mein Sohn
und zahl mir deine Schuldigkeit.
Ich, Leben, brauch den Tod,
ich, Zeit, die Ohnezeit.

Was plagst du dich,
da doch im Hellen steht
ein Liebesaug?
Du brauchst es nicht zu sehn.

Be mine son
and pay me down your debt.
I, Life, need Death,
I, Time, need Without-Time.

Why torment yourself,
when, after all, in brightness is set
an eye of love?
You don't need to see it.

Auf einem Tier, das raubt,
als in Träumen hängend.
Auf seinem Rücken
dämmernd denkend
umsonst, denn
das, was von selbst ist,
ist unergründlich,
wenn auch offenbar.

Zu schwach bist du,
das Geheimnis zu ehren,
irrst in der Unruh.
Doch Stille kommt
nach den Gedanken,
ursächlich.

On a beast that robs,
as if hanging in dreams.
On its back
dawning thinking
in vain, for ·
what is in itself
is unfathomable,
even if manifest.

You are too weak
to honor the secret;
you err in the restlessness.
But stillness comes
after thoughts,
causally.

Ende, das fertige,
ganz und gar jenseits
des Häuslichen, wo
Umgang war miteinander.

Was solls dann?
Freilich, das
entblutet ent-
blasene Hirn

ist ledig der Täuschung.
Blumen das Ähnlichste,
und Du kennst sie,
Du fragst

von ihnen aus nach dem Fragen,
sagst: es wisse, der gefragt hat,
der Getrennte, nichts mehr
von nichts,

geschweige vom Nichts.

The end, finished,
altogether beyond
the domestic, where
there was company.

So what, then?
Of course, the
de-blooded, de-
bloated brain

is unattached to pretense.
Flowers the most similar,
and you know them,
you ask

from where they are about asking,
saying: let him who asked,
the one separated, know nothing more
of nothing,

let alone of nothingness.

Im Zeitspalt
ein Gedanke gewesen,
bis der Ewigkeitsschrecken
ihn umwarf.

Was folgt,
ist nicht Schlaf,
sondern Skelett.

Das wissen
die Verständigen aber.

To have been a thought
in time's rift,
until the horror of eternity
overthrew it.

What follows
isn't sleep,
but skeleton.

But those who understand
know this.

Es will sich
im Toten
das Nichts verschweigen.
So ist es
ganz wirklich.

Nothingness wants
to conceal itself
in what is dead.
In this it is
quite real.

Auf das Ende sehen,
den Text ohne Wörter,
Worte führten dorthin
(fast bis dort),
sie hielten den Schritt an,
nein, sie erlahmten
im gräßlichen Gram
wegen alldem.

To look at the end,
the text without words,
some words led toward it
(almost to it),
they came to a halt,
no, they flagged
in awful grief
because of all that.

Tod: wie er sei.
Hohl, höhlenhohl
wär schon ein Bild
von Haus aus des Lebens.

Dies und
sein Ende
vermocht von den Menschen.

Das Gras hat es leichter.
Wir sind nicht wie Gras.

Death: how it might be.
Hollow, cavern-hollow
in itself already
would be an image of life.

This and
its end—
humanly possible.

The grass has it easier.
We are not like grass.

Ich kanns ermessen nun.
Es äußert sich
im Schwarm der Sonnen.

Genug ist das
und was hier Leiden heißt:
genug.

Ich braucht es nicht zu sehn,
vergessen werd ichs ja,
so Licht und Dunkel wie mein irdisch Hemd.

I can measure it now.
It expresses itself
in the swarm of suns.

That is enough
and what is here called suffering:
enough.

I didn't need to see it,
I'll forget it, of course,
as Light and Dark as my earthly shirt.

Gelesen dies:
»Unendlichkeit, tritt ein!«

Wie wär es möglich,
da sich das Endliche türmt?

Ich schau auf ein Fenster,
Himmelsviereck.

Noch bist du, Liebes,
meine Wohnung.

This was read:
"Infinity, come in!"

How would it be possible,
since the finite piles up?

I look at a window,
square of sky.

You, dear, are still
my dwelling.

Vorkommen lassen:
Des gesagten Einen
Mutwille ist es nicht.

Es tut nur, wie es kann,
vergibt, schränkt ein, merzt aus,
weiß nichts davon.

Die Offenheit ist groß,
verbirgt sich aber neu
in eines jeden Tod.

To allow to happen:
It is not the mischief
of the One mentioned.

It only acts in the way it can,
forgives, constricts, expunges,
knows nothing of it.

The openness is vast,
but it hides anew
in each and every death.

Von wo denn als
aus der Lust der Zeugung
kommt dieses Mißvergnügen?

Sag mir die Jahreszeit.

Die da verschwunden, die
Zeugenden, und ohne
Atem sind, was

geht sie der Seufzer noch an?

From where else does
this dissatisfaction come
than out of the delight of procreation?

Tell me the season.

Those who disappeared there, the
procreators, and who are
without breath, what

do they still care about the sigh?

Siehst dich an
als einen Fremdling
oft,

denn bald
tropfest du
von Verwesung,
scheinst zu ruhn.

You see yourself
as a stranger
often,
for before long
you'll drip
with rot,
appear to rest.

Totsein, welch
Leben, wirklich,
zusammen mit des Wurms
Eintönigkeit, stumm
den einstigen Esser zu essen.

(Der es erfunden hat,
jener Erfundene, das
schaurige Unten, sei
wahrlich der Höchste genannt.)

Wie war doch die Erde
gewürzt! Selbst bei
Ärmlichen gab es
Öl und Salz und die Frucht,
die ins Fenster hing . . .

To be dead, what
a life, really,
at one with the worm's
monotony, mutely
eating the erstwhile eater.

(The horrid beneath—
he who invented it,
himself invented, may
he truly be called the Highest.)

And how the dirt was
spiced! Even
the destitute had
oil and salt and the fruit
that hung in through the window . . .

Das vom Irdischen
Gewußte, noch lange
tönt's von Seiten
einiger Gerippe.
Wir ja, wir Bedürftigen,
wollen hören
das Lebende der Toten.

That which is known
of the terrestrial, it still
resounds on the part of
some skeletons.
We—we needy ones
want to hear
what is alive in the dead.

Im Notwendigen
welche Wendungen,
keine ist ohne Not.
Nur ein anderes steht da,
um, wenn du's anstößt,
sich wieder zu ändern.
Doch einmal verwandelt es sich
nicht mehr. Das Unentgehbare
hat statt. Die
Not bleibt stehn.

In need eternal
what turns—
none is without need.
Only an other stands there,
in order to change itself again,
whenever you jolt it.
But one time it transforms itself
no more. The unevadable
has place. Need
stands still.

Es kommt
unheilig längste Zeit,
wo das Geweb, das wahrgewobene,

sich in Erde ändert
und nichts mehr vorkommt
Augen oder Zunge.

Unzählige sind schon,
Kundige der Kunst,
ermattet in der Erde Riß.

Wenn sich das Korn,
das Erde heißt,
zerschliffen hat,

wer zeigt wem vor
ein letztes Bild?
Der Niemand steht am End.

The unholy longest time
is coming,
where the weave, the truth-woven,

changes into earth
and nothing else happens
eyes or tongue.

Countless are already,
art experts,
languishing in the earth's rip.

When the grain
that is called earth
has ground itself asunder,

who will show whom to
a last image?
The nobody stands at the end.

Hast du mir, Sonne,
oder habe ich dir
Augen gestohlen
in dem Augenblick,
wo mich, erloschen,
das All nichts mehr angeht?

Did you, sun, thieve
eyes from me,
or I from you,
in that moment's glance
when the universe no longer
concerns me, extinguished?

INDEX OF FIRST LINES

THE TRANSLATORS WOULD LIKE TO THANK
WILLIAM WATERS FOR HIS GENEROUS
ASSISTANCE AND JOSHUA BECKMAN FOR
HIS ENTHUSIASM AND ENCOURAGEMENT.